$15—

Joseph Brodsky
Leningrad

Also by Mikhail Lemkhin

Missing Frames

Joseph Brodsky

Leningrad

Fragments

Mikhail Lemkhin

Foreword by Czeslaw Milosz
Afterword by Susan Sontag

Farrar, Straus and Giroux
New York

Farrar, Straus and Giroux
19 Union Square West, New York 10003

Copyright © 1998 by Mikhail Lemkhin
Foreword copyright © 1998 by Czeslaw Milosz
Afterword copyright © 1998 by Susan Sontag
All rights reserved
Distributed in Canada by Douglas & McIntyre Ltd.
Printed in the United States of America
Designed by Monika Keano
First edition, 1998

Library of Congress Cataloging-in-Publication Data
Lemkhin, Mikhail, 1949-
    Fragments: Joseph Brodsky, Leningrad/Mikhail Lemkhin;
foreword by Czeslaw Milosz; afterword by Susan Sontag.
        p.   cm.
    ISBN 0-374-15831-2
    1. Brodsky, Joseph, 1940-1996—Pictorial works.
2. Brodsky, Joseph, 1940-1996—Homes and haunts—Russia
(Federation)—Saint Petersburg—Pictorial works. 3. Saint Petersburg
(Russia)—Pictorial works. I. Title
PG3479. 4. R64Z76   1998
811'. 54—dc 21
[B]   97-44215

contents

To my wife, Irina

foreword

Nothing in the twentieth century announced the appearance of a poet such as Brodsky. It was a century of revolutions coagulating into totalitarian systems; of monstrous wars and war crimes; of the erosions of traditional beliefs undermined by science and technology, as well as by the philosophies of Marx, Nietzsche, and Freud. A tremendous noise of screams, curses, and ideas combating each other mounted to the sky, filled every cubit of space. To all that, Joseph Brodsky opposed his vocation of a servant of the Muse, which meant that he wanted to serve the language. He said that a poet writes to please his predecessors, not his contemporaries.

A witness to and a participant in the turmoils of his century, he was affected by its disillusionments and despairs and yet managed to preserve his independence not only from the collectivistic political dogmas of Soviet society but also from a multitude of crazy proposals besieging minds in the West. Against all probability, the voice of a Russian poet pierced through the universal noise and was recognized in the world as a sober reminder of a hierarchy in arts and letters, a hierarchy above the fashions and follies of the day.

Brodsky was aware of his St. Petersburg heritage and, intellectually, was shaped in the first place by Dostoevsky—moreover, by Dostoevsky as interpreted by Lev Shestov. This influence fortified him against the rosy progressivism of much of nineteenth-century Russian literature and brought him closer to the Judeo-Christian tradition deeply embedded in the Russian language. Poems on subjects taken from the Old and the New Testaments are an important part of his oeuvre.

The surprising autonomy of Brodsky as a poet and a thinker finds its explanation not only in his personal gifts of mind and heart. His essays written in English testify to a rare erudition and, indirectly, prove that in his youth he succeeded in educating himself better than in any school. The young Leningrad poets in his group were voracious readers, explorers of libraries and secondhand bookshops in their city. Their effort at self-education was sustained in spite of unfavorable circumstances—or perhaps those circumstances were favorable because they allowed them to live in complete detachment from the way of thinking promoted by the state? These poets preserved a respect for freedom of judgment and today should be proud of Brodsky as one of their own.

In an epoch of disintegration and of bereavement, when all values mankind respected for centuries seem to be lost, a poet who wants to be a continuator is badly needed. Joseph Brodsky was not seduced by any avant-garde movements. Novelty in his poetry is solidly grounded in the language and ideas of poets who preceded him. He was a builder of bridges to the past—to the great periods of Russian poetry in the nineteenth and early twentieth centuries. Such a task also directed him to an older heritage, to Horace and Ovid.

Czeslaw Milosz

Fragments

People are what we remember about them. What we call life is in the end a patchwork of someone else's recollections. With death, it gets unstitched, and one ends up with random, disjointed fragments. With shards or, if you will, with snapshots. Filled with their unbearable laughter or equally unbearable smiles. Which are unbearable because they are one-dimensional. I should know; after all, I am a photographer's son. And I may even go as far as suggesting a link between picture taking and verse writing—well, insofar as the fragments are black-and-white. Or insofar as writing means retention.

—Joseph Brodsky, "In Memory of Stephen Spender"

For a man is what he loves. That's why he loves it: because he is a part of it.

—Joseph Brodsky, "Spoils of War"

14

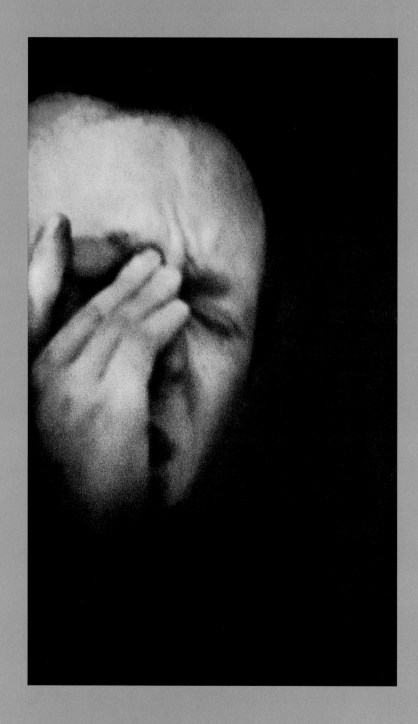

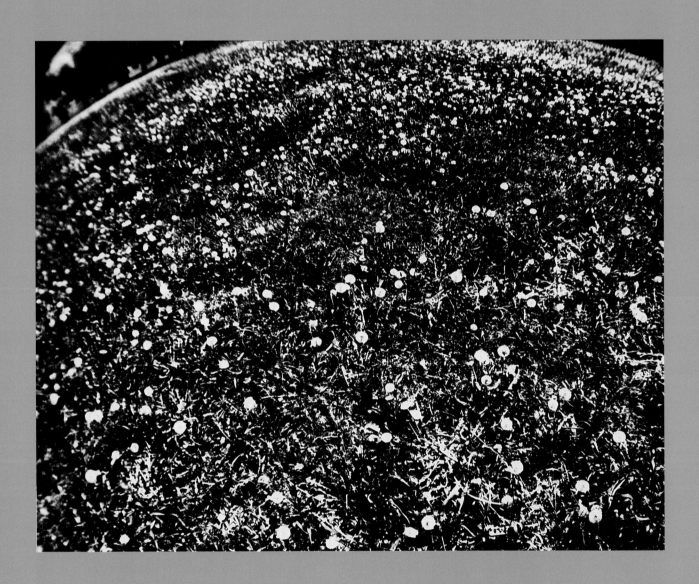

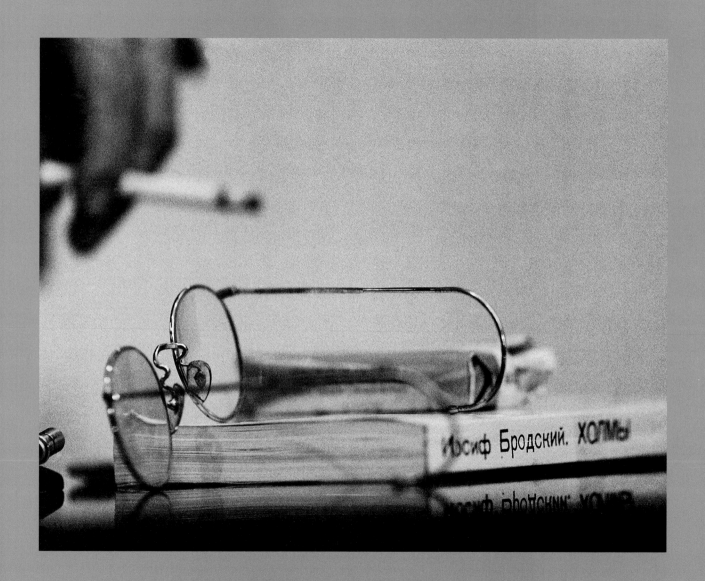

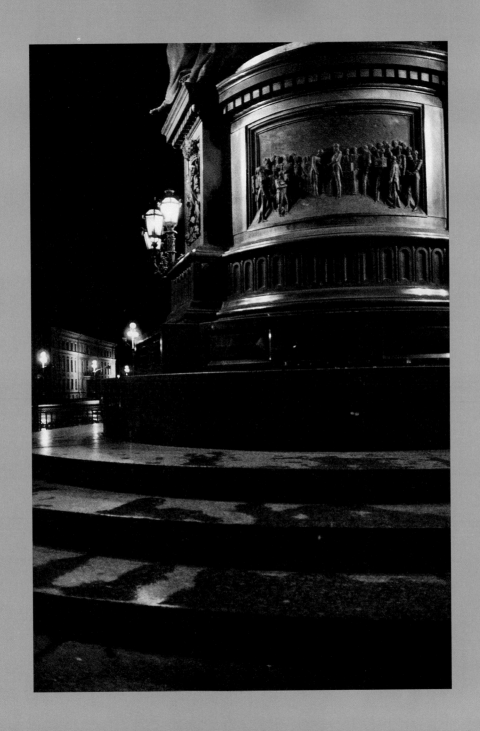

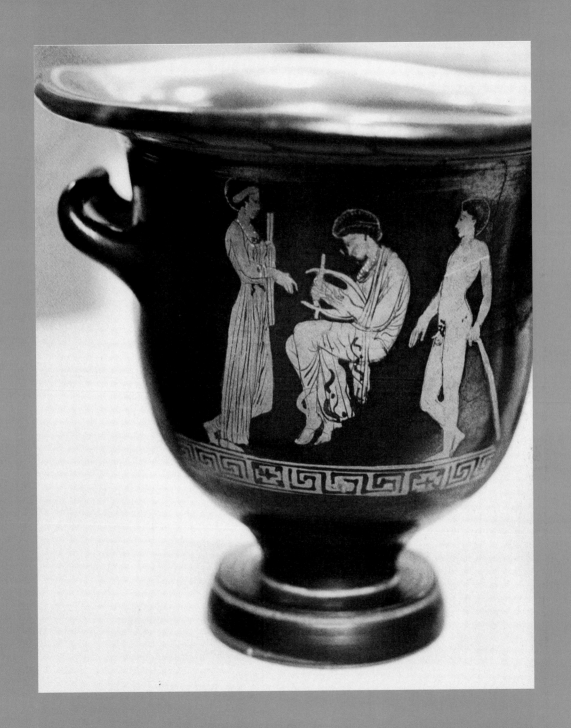

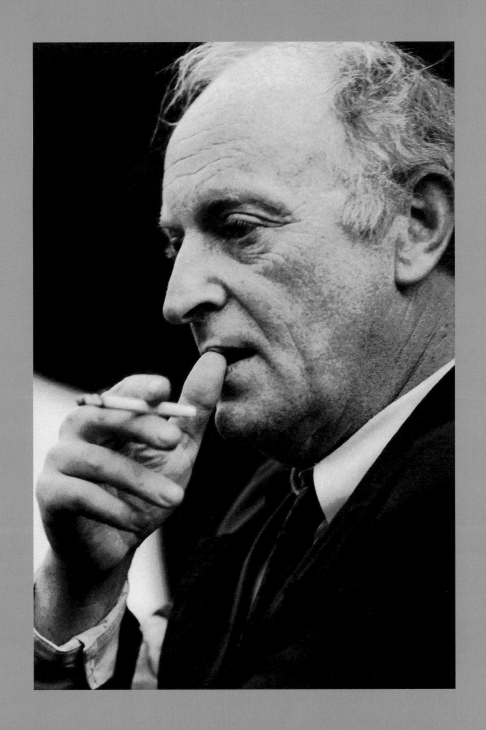

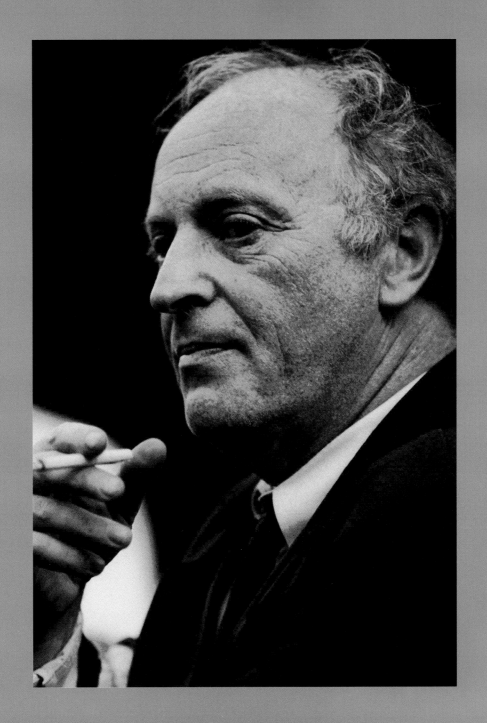

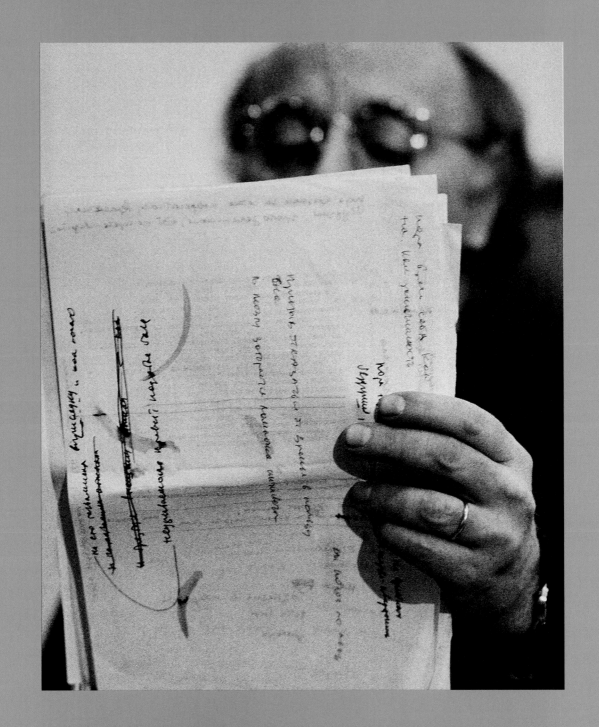

afterword

For as long as we *are*, we're always somewhere. Feet are always some-where, whether planted or running. Minds, notoriously, can be else-where. Minds, whether from lack of vitality or from the deepest strengths, can be in the past and the present, or the present and the future. Or simply here and there. For reasons not hard to understand, the making of art at the highest plane of accomplishment during the last century or so has required, more often than not, an exceptional devel-opment of the talent for being, mentally, in two places at once. Elated by the landscapes he has been painting and drawing in the South of France, van Gogh writes his brother Theo that he is "really" in Japan. The young, as yet unpublished poet from Leningrad fulfilling a sentence of compulsory labor on a collective farm in a village in the Far North, near the White Sea, receives the news—it is January 1965—that T. S. Eliot has died in London, sits at a table in his icy shack, and within the next twenty-four hours composes a long elegy to Eliot, which is also an homage to the very alive W. H. Auden (the tone and swing of whose elegy on the death of Yeats Brodsky adopts).

He was elegant enough always to claim that he had not really suffered during that year and a half of internal exile; that he rather liked farmwork, especially shoveling manure, which he regarded as one of the more honest and rewarding jobs he'd had so far, everyone in Russia being mired in shit, and had got quite a few poems written there.

Then, back in his native Leningrad, a few years later Joseph Brodsky, as he put it succinctly, "switched empires." This happened suddenly, from one day to the next, and entirely against his will: among other losses, it separated this beloved only son from his elderly parents, who, in further punishment of the renegade poet, were thereafter repeatedly denied exit permits by the Soviet government to meet for a brief reunion in, say, nearby Helsinki, and died without his ever embracing them again. Intractable grief, borne with great indignation, great sobriety.

He even managed to make of his KGB-enjoined departure something self-propelled—

And as for where in space and time one's toe end touches,
well, earth is hard all over; try the States

—landing among us like a missile hurled from the other empire, a benign missile whose payload was not only his genius but his native literature's exalted, exacting sense of the poet's authority. (To be found as well among its prose writers: think of how Gogol and Dostoevsky conceived of the novelist's moral and spiritual task.) Many aptitudes eased his rapid insertion in America: immense industriousness and self-confidence, ready irony, insouciance, cunning. But for all the dash and ingenuity of his connections with his adopted country, one had only to watch Joseph Brodsky among other Russian exiles and émigrés to realize how viscerally, expressively Russian he had stayed. And how generous his adaptation to us, along with the eagerness to impose himself on us, actually was.

Such adaptability, such gallantry, may go by the name of cosmopolitanism. But true cosmopolitanism is less a matter of one's relation to place than to time, specifically to the past (which is simply so much bigger than the present). This has nothing in common with that sentimental relation to the past called nostalgia. It is a relation, unsparing to oneself, which acknowledges the past as the source of standards, higher standards than the present affords. One should write to please not one's contemporaries but one's predecessors, Brodsky often declared. Surely he did please them—his compatriots agree that he was his era's unique successor to Mandelstam, Tsvetaeva, and Akhmatova. Raising the "plane of regard" (as he called it) was relentlessly identified with the effortfulness and ambitions and appropriate fidelities of poets.

I know Joseph Brodsky as a world poet—partly because I cannot read him in Russian; mainly because that's the range he commanded in his poems, with their extraordinary velocity and density of material notation, of cultural reference, of attitude. He insisted that poetry's "job" (a much-used word) was to explore the capacity of language to travel farther, faster. Poetry, he said, is accelerated thinking. It was his best argument, and he made many, on behalf of the superiority of poetry to prose, for he considered rhyme essential to this process. An ideal of mental acceleration is the key to his great achievement (and its limits), in prose as well as in poetry, and to his indelible presence. Conversation with him, as felicitously recalled by his friend Seamus Heaney, "attained immediate vertical takeoff and no deceleration was possible."

Much of his work could be subsumed under the early title of one of his poems, "Advice to a Traveller." Real travel nourished the mental journeying, with its characteristic premium on speedy assimilation of what there was to know and feel, determination never to be duped, rueful avowals of vulnerability. Of course, there were favorite elsewheres, four countries (and the poetry produced within their borders) in particular: Russia, England, America, and Italy. Which is to say, empires never ceased to incite his powers of fast-forward association and generalization; hence, his passion for the Latin poets and the sites of ancient Rome, inscribed in several essays and the play *Marbles* as well as in poems. The first, in the end perhaps the only tenable form of cosmopolitanism is to be a citizen of an empire. Brodsky's temperament was imperial in many senses.

Home was Russian. No longer Russia. Perhaps no decision he made in the later part of his life was as startling (to many), as emblematic of who he was, as his refusal, after the dismantling of the Soviet empire and in the face of countless worshipful solicitations, to go back even for the briefest visit.

And so he lived most of his adult life elsewhere: here. And Russia, the source of everything that was most subtle and audacious and fertile and doctrinaire about his mind and gifts, became the great elsewhere to which he could not, would not, out of pride, out of anger, out of anxiety, ever return.

Now he has rushed away from us, for so it feels, to reside in the largest, most powerful empire of all, the final elsewhere: a transfer whose anticipation (while enduring a serious cardiac ailment for many years) he explored in so many defiant, poignant poems.

The work, the example, the standards—and our grief—remain.

Susan Sontag

notes

Fragments is not just a photo album but a coherent whole—a photo-narrative or a photo-poem. The book contains 186 photographs; some are images of Joseph Brodsky and some are of the city of Leningrad (as it was called from 1924 to 1991). But, rather than a collection of images, *Fragments* is a *single portrait*. Each photo is like a word or a phrase I use to tell my story, to sketch my subject's portrait.

I believe that my photo-poem, like any other novel, poem, or story, does not require extensive footnoting. If an author manages to find the right intonation, if a reader or viewer can hear the author's voice and feel the rhythm of his speech, then an unfamiliar word will not break the tissue of the narrative. Conversely, if an author undertakes to comment on what he meant here and what he meant there, then that type of annotation would quickly destroy his intonation, and, paradoxically, the new information would diminish rather than increase the author's contact with the reader.

If, however, that which every author dreams about occurs—if a reader, trusting the author, turns the last page and feels a sudden urge to go back to the beginning, then I feel the need to explain a few facts about a remote way of life and an unfamiliar tongue. To such a reader, I offer a modest number of notes.

Why did I choose to footnote these particular images and circumstances, and not comment on the many other historic sights and cultural facts? The reader is entitled to ask this question, but I am afraid that I have no clear answer. I do not claim that these notes are scholarly annotations, and they are certainly not a set of cultural tips for tourists. My only concern is to preserve the emotional tonality of my narrative.

—*Mikhail Lemkhin*

Page 22. A sign hanging on the staircase landing opposite Brodsky's Leningrad apartment calls for the recycling of "paper, ivory, old rubber shoes, ferrous and nonferrous metals, mattress stuffing."

Page 23. The building at the corner of Liteiny Prospect and Pestel Street, in which Brodsky lived from about 1952 until his departure from the U.S.S.R. in 1972. Built for Prince Alexander Muruzi, it is known as the Muruzi House.

Page 35. The sphinx's features are those of the pharaoh Amenhotep III (1417-1379 B.C.). Taken from the pharaoh's mortuary temple in Egypt, the sphinx was delivered to St. Petersburg in the spring of 1832 and placed on the embankment of the Neva River.

Pages 40, 186. The building that housed the Stock Exchange before the October 1917 Revolution. In 1940, it became the Central Navy Museum, where Brodsky's father worked in the photography department.

Page 41. The foyer and staircase to Brodsky's apartment.

Page 42. The same foyer, from the main entrance. On the wall is a peculiar kind of official graffiti: "If you smell gas, dial 01."

Page 43. New Holland—one of the forty-two islands upon which St. Petersburg stands. These islands are

formed by sixty-eight rivers, tributaries, and canals, and are connected by 539 bridges. St. Petersburg has more bridges than Amsterdam, Stockholm, or Venice, also famous for their bridges.

Page 54. Brodsky reading from his book *The End of a Beautiful Era*.

Pages 55, 121, 123. The Jewish Cemetery, on the southeastern edge of the city. The graves of Brodsky's parents are here.

Page 56. A window in Brodsky's apartment.

Page 57. Brodsky's entrance to his apartment building.

Page 61. One of the most notorious buildings in Leningrad, located a few blocks from Brodsky's apartment—the Leningrad headquarters of the KGB. Leningraders popularly referred to it as the Big House. Brodsky was interrogated here.

Pages 64, 183. The Alexandrine Column. A Doric column carved from a gigantic block of granite, with a bronze base and bronze bas-reliefs on its pedestal, crowned by the statue of an angel. It was erected in Palace Square in front of the Winter Palace in 1830-34, to commemorate the victory of Alexander I over Napoleon in the War of 1812. The tallest monolithic pillar in the world, it measures 156 feet from pedestal to summit.

In Russia, even those who have never been to St. Petersburg, or who have not seen a picture of the column, are familiar with these lines of Alexander Pushkin's written in 1836:

A monument to myself, made not with hand I've builded,
   To which the people's path shan't come to be o'ergrown;
      Higher skyward rose its front to loom, its will unyielded,
         O'er Alexander's pillar of stone.*

Pages 68, 110. Overlooking the Fontanka River from the Egyptian Bridge, an iron sphinx created in 1825 by the sculptor Pavel Sokolov.

Pages 79, 80. Crosses prison, where Brodsky was incarcerated in 1964.

Page 96. Cathedral of Fyodorovsky Madonna, built to commemorate the tercentennary of the Romanov dynasty. Dedicated on January 15, 1914, it continued to serve as a church even after the October 1917 Revolution, until, in 1932, it was turned into a dairy.

Page 104. View of Pestel Street from Brodsky's balcony.

Pages 105, 198. St. Panteleimon's Church, down the street from the house where Brodsky lived, could be seen from his balcony.

Page 110. The sign above the feet of the sphinx proclaims: "Long live the Soviet Union!"

Pages 112, 114. Fyodor Dostoevsky's tombstone in the cemetery of the Alexander Nevsky Monastery.

Pages 124, 142, 161. Eighteenth-century Italian sculptures in the Summer Garden.

Page 149. The sign on the door reads: "Department of Construction Management."

Page 151. The house built in 1791 by the architect Nikolai Lvov for the poet and cabinet minister Graviil Derzhavin. Derzhavin's study was in the bay of the second story of the house.

Pages 175, 177. The Fortress of Peter and Paul, begun in 1703. It was a fort, a prison, and a burial vault for Russian emperors; now it is a museum. On July 13, 1826, five leaders of the Decembrist anti-government uprising were executed in the fortress. Among them was the poet Kondraty Ryleev.

*"Unto Myself I Reared a Monument," translated by Nathan Lemkhin.

acknowledgments

I would like to thank my friends for their help and advice: Elena and Yury Alexandrov, Andrei Ariev, Yakov Gordin, Mikhail Iampolski, Otar Iosseliany, Lev Loseff, Helen and Joseph Ostashevsky, Andrey Pinaev, Georgy Shablovsky, Alexandr Volpert, Vladimir Ufland; and my son, Nathan Lemkhin.

I wish to express my gratitude to Czeslaw Milosz, Susan Sontag, and Roger W. Straus for believing in my work.

My special thanks to Cachet Fine Art Photographic Paper Company for their generous support in helping me to bring this project to fruition.

—M.L.